Avoid Negative People and Situations

I carefully choose the people I allow into my life.

I am in control of my life, and one way I exercise control is by being selective of the people I allow to be part of it.

I know that some people have the ability to create drama and drain my resources. I avoid these people so that I can have an enjoyable life. Negative people are unwelcome in my life.

I also do my best to avoid negative situations. The things that happen in my life are sometimes outside of my control, but I reject negative situations. I avoid situations that make my life more challenging unnecessarily. I actively remove negative people and situations whenever possible.

I maintain high standards in my life. I am willing to let go of the people and situations that fail to serve me or support my dreams. I am a positive person, and I love to be around others who are positive.

What are the negative situations in my life?

Why are these situations in my life?

Who are the negative people in my life?

Why are they part of my life?

What can I do to avoid negative people and situations?

Believe in the Healing Power of Forgiveness

I forgive myself for any mistakes in judgment and use the experience to learn.

I release any lingering resentment or anger toward myself, focusing only on healing.

When I have a negative experience, I go back to the source to understand how I created those feelings.

I allow myself to heal.

I open my mind and heart to receive new knowledge from my experiences. I use my intuition to guide me. I ask myself what I can learn and move forward.

I allow myself to feel the pain of the past, and I forgive the past experiences that led me here so that I may let go of it and grow stronger.

I forgive myself if I feel angry or resentful, especially if I have an attachment to outcomes. Instead, I am compassionate, and I let go.

In what ways do I hold onto negative beliefs
about myself?

How does this affect my daily life?

How can I forgive myself for holding these beliefs?

_____

_____

_____

_____

_____

_____

_____

_____

_____

_____

_____

_____

Celebrate Life With Each Breath

I choose to see the magnificence in the small things. I am grateful for this life.

I have come to the understanding that each moment is precious. I only get one chance to experience the wonders of each moment, so I take advantage of the opportunity to find joy in a present moment mindset.

I realize that, just as the sunset is fleeting, so is my life.

I notice the small things. I pick up feathers on the ground to remind me of Heaven. I notice the puffy clouds against the pale blue sky and marvel at their beauty. I stare at the rainbows made from cut crystal in my window.

I am starting to appreciate life more. I am starting to appreciate people more. I am starting to appreciate my breath even more.

With each moment of appreciation, I notice that I receive more to appreciate. With each moment of gratitude, I get more to be grateful for.

With each moment of splendor, I see even more as I stand in utter awe of life.

I choose to have more fun in each moment. I choose to find the "funny" in my blunders. I laugh at my mistakes and missteps. I get up, brush myself off, and make a joke about it.

I create events to celebrate. I call up friends and tell them how much I appreciate them. I create gatherings to truly connect with like-minded people.

What has changed about your life, your home, your work, and your family that you could not have imagined a year ago?

How would you describe your life as a journey?

_____

_____

_____

_____

_____

_____

_____

_____

_____

_____

_____

_____

Determined

to

Succeed

I am ambitious. I set specific goals. I know what I want out of life.

My vision and priorities are clear. I put my targets into writing and keep them in the front of my mind. I take action and measure my progress.

I persevere through obstacles. I remember that life is full of ups and downs. I control how I respond to situations. When I experience a setback, I develop alternative strategies.

I take risks. I embrace change and learn from experience. I dream big and try new things.

I remember my purpose. I focus on the reasons behind my activities. I trust my instincts and follow my passions. I make decisions that align with my core values and beliefs.

Today, I pursue my personal definition of success. I have courage and commitment. I am excited about my opportunities and confident in my abilities.

What does success mean to me?

Where do I find inspiration?

What makes me unstoppable?

_____

_____

_____

_____

_____

_____

_____

_____

_____

_____

_____

_____

_____

Empathy

Builds

Humility

I stand in solidarity with my brothers and sisters around me. Understanding their realities educates me on how to stand in defense of their causes.

When I actively listen to the plight of others, I gain a greater sense of the challenges that they face. I sincerely connect with their feelings by putting myself in their shoes. The way forward is much clearer to me when I do that.

I am able to lend a hand to someone who I love by carefully understanding their situation. My support is rooted in common knowledge and connected emotions.

The difficulties that my friends face feel more personal to me when I take the time to connect with them emotionally. I am reminded that even when I feel like things are tough, there is always someone who is having a tougher time.

Shifting perspectives challenges what I am conditioned to think. It allows me to come face to face with my own privilege and practice humility.

Thinking about what someone else is going through takes me away from focusing on myself. Although I have my own challenges, it is important to think wider than my own reality. I learn valuable life lessons by embracing others in their difficult times.

When I tell someone that I understand how they feel, I say it with meaning. That meaning comes from stepping out of my shoes and into theirs.

How often do I practice empathy?
How often do I call on my loved ones when
I feel like being listened to?
What does empathy look like when
someone experiences tragedy?

_____

_____

_____

_____

_____

_____

_____

_____

_____

_____

_____

_____

Forgive Myself

I choose a life free from self-judgment, I accept myself as I am without needing to be anything else. I choose to love myself just the way I am.

I choose to believe that I deserve to be happy. I prefer to trust that I can become a better person because I learn so much through the process of healing.

I forgive myself completely for any acts of sabotage that caused me to feel unworthy or unlovable.

I forgive myself for giving away my power to anyone else.

I forgive myself for using food, drink, drugs, sex, money, or anything to satisfy my needs instead of trusting my true desires.

I forgive myself and align my agenda with loving myself completely. I forgive myself and believe I am worthy of happiness.

I forgive myself wholeheartedly, and I know I belong.

I forgive myself compassionately, and I forgive my parents, siblings, and loved ones.

Today, I forgive myself entirely and accept myself as I truly am. I forgive myself wholly and vow to live my truth. I forgive myself fully and acknowledge the illusion of control in my life.

What makes forgiveness a powerful tool?

How do I feel as I forgive myself?

What does it feel like to forgive others?

_____

_____

_____

_____

_____

_____

_____

_____

_____

_____

_____

_____

GROW

Grow in Wisdom and Strength Each Day

As each day passes, I learn more about myself and the world. I trust my instincts and my insight to guide me to positive choices. I am strong enough to walk away from harmful options.

I put the knowledge that I acquire each day to good use. I learn from my own shortcomings and the mistakes of others. I have the courage to admit when I am wrong and the strength to change course should I find myself on the wrong path.

I have sound judgment and a clear mind. I am brave. I trust my ability to make wise decisions. I have confidence that I can choose a positive direction for my life.

I am free of my mistakes of the past. I learn from my errors and grow wiser and each day.

I have a discerning spirit. I am observant of the people and events around me. Although I am patient and kind with others, I am not easily swayed or misled.

I am wise enough to know that I still have many things to learn about myself, others, and the universe. I am strong enough to embrace the wisdom that my life experiences can teach me.

Today, I give thanks for my wisdom and strength. I welcome my continued growth as I become wiser and more courageous each day.

What have I learned from the times I made unwise decisions?

What steps can I take to grow in knowledge and strength?

Who can mentor me in my quest to become wiser?

_____

_____

_____

_____

_____

_____

_____

_____

_____

_____

_____

_____

_____

Help

Others

I learn through trial and error how to best help others. I try to see things from another person's point of view. I try to put myself in their shoes. I try to understand how they might feel and why they may think or behave as they do.

Through learning with others, I understand myself. I become more patient, flexible, and understanding. I know empathy and compassion.

I learn to love myself enough to accept others.

When I help someone else, it makes me happy and strengthens my own sense of wellbeing.

By helping someone else, I am giving back to my fellow human beings. This gives me tremendous satisfaction. It fills my heart with joy.

When I assist another person, I feel less burdened. When I am free of burden, I have the energy to help someone else, and this inspires me to help more people. I grow stronger as I help others.

Today, I am learning how to love myself and others unconditionally. I am discovering that the more I show myself love and compassion, the more love and compassion I extend toward others as well. I grow in strength, confidence, and wellbeing as I help others.

How does helping others benefit me?

Could I be less selfish and more generous?

Am I willing to admit that I need help sometimes?

_____

_____

_____

_____

_____

_____

_____

_____

_____

_____

_____

_____

Influence
for
Good

I choose to be a positive influence in the world. I can see where the old rules are disintegrating, so I choose to create a new world. Where there is greed, I teach the art of sharing. Where there is misuse of power, I come from a compassionate heart. Where there is dishonesty, I speak from my Soul.

I am entering a new era of peace. When I walk in the room, I bring a peaceful presence. I stand for integrity at all times and in all places. I refuse to compromise my values or ethics. I stand in my truth. I set impeccable boundaries. I am invincible in my convictions.

I rid my mind of clutter. I let go of old, worn out beliefs. I reduce unnecessary time wasters. I feel clean and unencumbered.

By being brave and facing my fears head on, I have risen triumphantly! Like a hot air balloon who leaves bags of sand on the ground, I flow with the winds of life. I feel free. I feel lighter. I feel more genuinely my authentic self. I have my inner light to guide me.

By being a genuine, caring human being, I can care for others while also taking care of myself first.

Today, I am clear with my boundaries, and others see that strength as I become a more powerful influencer for good.

How can I be an influencer of good in the world?

Where can my influence be best served?

Who's lives can I influence?

_____

_____

_____

_____

_____

_____

_____

_____

_____

_____

_____

_____

_____

Joy is a Choice

There is great joy in the little things in life.

Little things make me laugh and bring me great joy. Joyous events of great magnitude make me happy, of course, but the small events add up in life and become the foundation of what brings me happiness and peace.

I partake in the little joys that happen around me each day. If I look around, I can always find something to be joyful about in that moment.

Joy is a choice. Because I know I control my own destiny, I choose to be joyful and happy.

By taking joy from the little things, I am rarely disappointed. There is always something nearby that makes me happy. I like to live a simple life where small things matter each day. I share that philosophy and my joy with other people, so they can have joy in their lives.

By sharing my joy of little things with others, I am even happier. The joy I send out radiates back to me in everything I do. People appreciate my simple joy. People find more joy in their own lives when I am around.

I show people how to appreciate the little things in life, and it makes their lives better. By working to make my life more joyful, I am able to share more joy with others. There is great power in great joy.

Today, I take the time to reflect on the little things in life that make me smile.

List some memories that made me feel joy?

What can I do to bring more joy into my life?

Why do I sometimes hold myself back from

being happy?

_____

_____

_____

_____

_____

_____

_____

_____

_____

_____

_____

_____

KEEP

Keep Promises That I Make To Myself

How I treat myself is an indicator of how I handle relationships with others. Giving myself the same treatment that I give to my loved ones is important to my self-worth.

My daily promise is to be kind to myself. Even when I make a silly mistake, I refrain from calling myself unkind names.

It is important for me to love the reflection that I see in the mirror. Doing this keeps me inspired. I tell myself that regardless of the situation, I believe in my ability to overcome. Constant self-belief keeps me from giving up.

One of my biggest promises is to make time for relaxation. Although work comes my way consistently, I only do what I am able to do in a given day.

A complete day involves stepping back from the work routine and unwinding. I promise to get pampered or treat myself to a nice dinner each day. It puts a smile on my face to experience the goodness that I show to others.

Achieving financial discipline is a challenge for me, but it is an important endeavor. Giving up on achieving it is hardly an option. I tell myself each day that my spending habits determine my ability to hit that target. Then I promise myself to maintain a healthy relationship with money.

Today, taking care of myself gives me the ability to take care of others. I treat myself with goodness and honesty because I deserve it. My promise is to remember that.

What do I promise myself at the end of each day?

Which promises to myself do I break?

What changes in my life do I need to make in order to keep the promises I made?

_____

_____

_____

_____

_____

_____

_____

_____

_____

_____

_____

_____

Listen To
My Intuition

I am finally giving my intuition a chance to be heard. I have confidence enough in my inner voice to give it a chance to speak up.

I listen attentively now, as I know it brings forth my greatest wisdom. I realize that my truth may not be the same as other people's truth, and I am okay with that.

I have tamed my ego. I feel more balanced now that I give equal time to my intuition and my intellect. My intuition is actually smarter. I make better decisions when I listen to my heart.

The more I stay grounded in my truth, the better my life becomes. I am more honest with myself. I am humbler. I am becoming wiser. I feel my highest truths coming forth.

I start to journal this newfound wisdom. I listen to my highest guidance. I still my mind and new information from my wisdom starts pouring in.

I take the time to quiet my thoughts. I walk outdoors in nature. I breathe a breath of fresh air. I calm down. I take time for stillness. I feel myself relaxing into my true authentic self.

Today, I listen to my intuition. I find peace within. I realize I am more than what I have become in the outer world. I am whole.

What do I need to do to create more stillness in my life?
What is my intuition teaching me?
What truths are being revealed that I need to pay attention to now?

_____

_____

_____

_____

_____

_____

_____

_____

_____

_____

_____

_____

Motivate

Myself

I am driven to succeed.

I remember my purpose. Thinking about the reasons behind my activities makes me want to push myself.

I boost my energy level. I take a walk around the block or do a few pushups. I play upbeat music and sing out loud. I enjoy a few deep breaths or share a laugh with a friend.

I give myself a pep talk. I review my past achievements. I recognize my progress and congratulate myself for making an effort. I reassure myself when I run into obstacles. I treat myself with compassion and accept ups and downs as a natural part of life.

I take breaks. I give myself time to rest and recharge.

I collaborate with others. My motivation grows even stronger when I surround myself with others who share my passions.

I set goals that are exciting and realistic for me. I go after what I want. I take one step forward. I find something I can accomplish immediately. I build momentum that carries me forward.

I think positive. I tell myself that I can do this.

Today, I am eager to seize opportunities and persevere until I succeed. My motivation comes from within

What can I do when my motivation starts to sink?

How does my diet affect my motivation?

How does gratitude help me to stay motivated?

_____

_____

_____

_____

_____

_____

_____

_____

_____

_____

_____

_____

New Life
Begins Today

Today is the first day of the rest of my life. I am finally beginning to live the life I was destined to live. I refuse to allow anything to stand in my way. Today is the day it happens!

Today is the day that everything changes for the better.

I understand the value of each day. I respect and cherish every day of my life.

I am determined to live my life in a way that pleases me. I am committed to living a life that demonstrates my preferences and values.

I am starting a new chapter in my life that suits me perfectly.

I make myself a priority starting today. I have plans for how I want to live my life, and they become a reality today.

I am taking responsibility for the life I live. I am a change-maker, and I am making things happen! I know what needs to be done, and I am doing it.

I refuse to allow anything to stop me. I am committed to the future that I desire.

Today, I start my new life. I am living my life differently than before. I am now living the life that is best for me.

How would I describe the kind of life I want to live?
What is stopping me?
Why have I allowed myself to continue living a life
 I don't enjoy fully?
What can I change today that will bring me closer to
living the ideal life for me?

_____

_____

_____

_____

_____

_____

_____

_____

_____

_____

_____

_____

Open the Window of Opportunity

I let the light of new beginnings flow into my space. I fling the curtains of doubt open and receive new inspiration!

I actively avoid closing myself off from opportunity. I open up my heart. I breathe in the new beginnings!

I release old patterns of self-sabotage. I gratefully say goodbye to all the limiting beliefs from my past. I dust off the doubt dirt from my shoes and get ready to polish them for what is next!

I buy new clothes that fit my new look. I reinvent myself. I see myself in a whole new light.

I stand tall in my new suit of clothing. I feel confidence shining through. I put on my happy face. I feel my new "me" starting to expand and shine outward.

I expand my thinking to what is my next best step. I boldly stride forward into my future.

I have unlimited opportunities laid at my feet!

I shine with newfound strength. I polish up my attitude. I create my new look.

Now that I have released all those shabby, old thoughts and beliefs, I feel my energy expand. I feel strong, happy, and confident.

Today, I know I can do anything I put my mind to. I am excited about my future. I feel great things are coming through my open window of opportunity and landing in my lap of happiness!

What old, worn-out beliefs need to be thrown out now?

What can I do to polish up my new image?

How can I reflect my new "Me" both internally and externally?

Protect

My

Space

I do this in all areas of my life. I am excellent at setting boundaries.

The older I get, the more I realize who I am. I am getting extremely clear about what is important to me. I realize that I need to set effective boundaries in order for others to respect my space.

I am clear with my communication. I ensure that everyone knows what appropriate behavior in my space is. I teach them to be respectful of my space, which then teaches them the importance of respecting their own space.

I am seeing where in the past, if I was unclear with my boundaries, they were often overlooked. I now take responsibility for being clear with my communication on all levels.

As I show more respect towards myself, I am shown more respect from others. I also want to respect the boundaries of others and ask curious questions to ensure that I act appropriately.

I set appropriate boundaries from a place of kindness. I smile and use positive words to show proper behavior around me. I use all my speaking skills to the best of my ability.

I practice my body language. I observe other people's body language. I listen attentively to others. I listen attentively to my own language patterns and modify my voice to be kind.

Today, I exhibit respectful behavior at work and at home. I make creating excellent boundaries a fun exercise in positive communication.

How can I show others respectful boundary skills?

How can I strengthen my communication skills?

Where could I create more effective boundaries in my life?

_____

_____

_____

_____

_____

_____

_____

_____

_____

_____

_____

_____

Quote of The Day

Fill this Page With Your Favorite Inspirational Quotes

Pick a quote that describes how you feel today. Write it down and discuss how it fits your mood. Make a case for why you picked that specific quote —consider wording, imagery, etc.

Replace Fear With Faith

In these unprecedented times, it is imperative that I pay attention to my emotional states. I realize how easily it is to be triggered at this time. I let go of those emotions that fail to support me, such as fear, and usher in faith, instead.

I constantly monitor my thoughts and feelings. I take a barometer reading of where I am on the happiness scale. I move the dial up when it gets below neutral.

I choose to unplug from the negative news. I choose to take a break from social media. I let go of people in my life who try to bring me down.

I let go of my addiction to controversial subjects. I let go of the constant bantering of political media. I turn off my television and computer. I take a break from the external world.

I choose to spend my time in nature. I walk my dog. I sit by a tree. I go barefoot in the grass. I read uplifting books. I subscribe to positive publications. I find positive people to have congenial conversations with.

I find positive ways of using my time. I use exercise programs that fulfill me. I choose healthy foods. I notice what lifts me up and I do more of that. I find positive articles that support my faith in life.

Today, I recite positive affirmations throughout the day. I feel my mood improving each moment. I am on my path from fear into faith.

What can I do to strengthen my faith?
Who can I talk with who will help lift me up?
How can I be an example of someone who has overcome
fear and applies faith principles to their life?

_____

_____

_____

_____

_____

_____

_____

_____

_____

_____

_____

Sow Seeds of Truth, Compassion & Understanding

I choose to sow seeds of positivity into the field of unlimited possibilities. I have grown a great deal this year, and it is time to sow these learnings back into the ground to replenish the earth.

I take the time to sow good seeds.

I choose to do good deeds. I am kind and generous with my harvest.

I open my heart and pocketbook to those in need. I share what I have. I spread the joy of life into the collective consciousness.

I do my part to make this world a better place.

I think good thoughts and sow those out into the world. I know that thoughts create things. I choose to create good things.

I help my neighbor. I comfort a friend. I reach out to those who are less fortunate and do what I can to help.

I bring a smile to work. I find something funny to share on the internet. I sow seeds of truth where people are open to listen.

Today, everywhere I go, I intentionally bring joy and happiness to each encounter. I do what I can to cultivate my garden with truth, compassion, and understanding. I know that I reap what I sow, and I choose to sow good seeds of positivity.

Where can I sow seeds of compassion?
Where can I sow seeds of understanding?
Where can I gently sow seeds of truth
for those who are searching and open?

_____

_____

_____

_____

_____

_____

_____

_____

_____

_____

_____

_____

Tap into the Universal Presence

I take the time to be one with the universal presence. By being present to all that is, I am aware of things that I would like to let go of. I can heal past traumas.

I notice amazing things about myself that I am ready to bring forth. The more present I am, the faster I can process through old behavior.

I have expanded my awareness, and everything is happening at once. I feel like, for a moment, I am able to stop, slow down, or speed up time. I have entered into timelessness.

I have entered the zone. I can savor the things that are really meaningful and dismiss the things that are irrelevant. I am present in the Presence.

With this newfound magic wand, I can enjoy my life exponentially. I enjoy food on a whole new level. I realize guilt is a useless emotion. I dispel it from my reality. Poof. It is gone.

I realize that I am MAGICAL! I can create anything I want. I can live my life FULL OUT! I expand my capacity to breathe in LIFE!

Today, I feel like I can see everything clearly on all levels. All my senses are in a state of expanded joy and bliss. I am blessed beyond measure.

How can I expand my capacity for more joy?
How can I expand my capacity for more peace?
How can I expand my capacity for greater bliss?

Unleash
My
Potential

I am strong and successful. I make choices that align with my values. I slow down and focus on one task at a time. I take refreshing breaks throughout the day.

I build my capabilities. I continue to grow personally and professionally. I read books and listen to podcasts. I take courses online.

I manage my time. I plan my schedule in advance. I block out time for my priority projects. I limit distractions, like watching TV or social media.

I adopt healthy habits. I maintain my energy by eating a nutritious diet, exercising regularly, and sleeping well.

I persevere through obstacles. I am committed to reaching my goals, even when I run into disappointments and delays. I learn from experience. I experiment with different strategies.

I surround myself with support. I spend time with family and friends who give me practical assistance and moral encouragement. I use gentle and inspirational words when I talk to myself.

I evaluate my progress and celebrate each victory.

I try new things. I push myself beyond my comfort zone. My doubts and fears fade away when I face them head on.

Today, I work hard and stay positive. Striving to fulfill my potential gives my life more meaning. I feel happy and content.

What are some activities that stimulate my personal growth?

What is one important thing that I learned this past year?

Why is personal development a lifelong process?

VALUE

Value
My
Time

Time is a valuable commodity. I am learning to apply excellent time management skills.

I am grateful for the time I have here on this Earth. I realize I am only here for a short duration. Due to that fact, I am extremely aware of time management.

I take all the time I need to evaluate what is worth my time. I schedule time in my life for all my priorities. I take a look at what is precious to me and order my time schedule accordingly.

I reprioritize my time according to what is most important, somewhat important and minimally important. I ensure that I schedule time for myself, as I am my most important commodity.

I use good time management skills for my time off as well. I give generously to my down time. I know that replenishing the well is necessary in order to nourish my garden.

I take time when I get home to play with my dog. I greet my family with love. I sit down and enjoy a healthy meal. I get plenty of rest.

I am excellent at creating work/life balance. I am enjoying my time off more. I leave all my work worries at the office. I leave my home problems at home.

I do what is necessary to resolve my issues. I take care of my mental and emotional health.

Today, I am proud of how well I manage my time. I understand how important my time is and schedule my life accordingly.

How can I manage my time better?

Where can I cut out unnecessary time wasters?

Which priorities do I want to spend more time with?

How can I add this to my schedule?

Write Down My Goals

I know what I want and how to achieve it. Putting my goals on paper clarifies my thinking and increases my motivation. I deepen my sense of commitment. I feel more accountable. I am less likely to become distracted or make excuses.

I create clear and compelling language. I ensure that my goals are meaningful and realistic for me. I add details and descriptions that help me to translate my objectives into concrete steps.

I focus on what I can control. I design goals that depend on my effort and resources rather than counting on external events.

I post my goals where I can see them. I keep a copy on my phone and inside my office door. My targets stay fresh in my mind.

I check off the tasks as I complete them. Each accomplishment gives me satisfaction and helps me to build more momentum. I feel confident in myself and my abilities. I know that I can realize my dreams.

Today, I am determined to succeed. I expand my comfort zone and create the results I want. I keep my goals in sight.

WELLBEING WEEKLY GOALS

Living by Giving:
What act of kindness will you complete this week?

Learning and Trying:

What goal are you going to try and accomplish this week?

Purposeful Praise:
How will you make another person feel appreciated?

Reflecting and Acknowledging:
What are you proud of achieving this week?

WELLBEING WEEKLY GOALS CONT...

Living by Giving:

Learning and Trying:

Purposeful Praise:

Reflecting and Acknowledging:

WELLBEING WEEKLY GOALS CONT...

Living by Giving:

Learning and Trying:

Purposeful Praise:

Reflecting and Acknowledging:

WELLBEING WEEKLY GOALS CONT...

Living by Giving:

Learning and Trying:

Purposeful Praise:

Reflecting and Acknowledging:

GOAL WORKSHEET

GOAL:

WHY?

STEPS TO TAKE

- _____
- _____
- _____
- _____

NOTES

_____

_____

_____

_____

GOAL WORKSHEET

GOAL:

WHY?

STEPS TO TAKE

- _____
- _____
- _____
- _____

NOTES

_____
_____
_____
_____

GOAL WORKSHEET

GOAL:

WHY?

STEPS TO TAKE

- _____
- _____
- _____
- _____

NOTES

_____
_____
_____
_____

GOAL WORKSHEET

GOAL:

WHY?

STEPS TO TAKE

- _____
- _____
- _____
- _____

NOTES

_____

_____

_____

_____

What makes you excited?

What makes you feel young at heart?

Write a letter to your younger self.

What words of wisdom do you have

for yourself?

_____

_____

_____

_____

_____

_____

_____

_____

_____

_____

_____

_____

ZEN

List things that make you feel calm:

ZEN ACTIVITY LIST

When you feel your stress levels building up try this!!!

- [ ] Stretch or try Yoga
- [ ] Spend a day at the pool
- [ ] Read a book
- [ ] Practice progressive muscle relaxation
- [ ] Go for a walk
- [ ] Get a massage
- [ ] Write down your worries
- [ ] Color a Mandala
- [ ] Try essential oils and aromatherapy
- [ ] Watch a Comedy Special on TV or go to a show
- [ ] Create a garden
- [ ] Listen to live music

Self Regulation Ideas
Before I explode, I will

Circle some ideas you will try.

Get a drink	Draw a picture	Take calming breaths
Take a walk	Talk with someone	Take a break

What helped you calm down today? _____

_____

_____

_____

_____

_____

_____

What are the negative situations in my life?
Why are these situations in my life?
Who are the negative people in my life?
Why are they part of my life?
What can I do to avoid negative people and situations?

_____

_____

_____

_____

_____

_____

_____

_____

_____

_____

_____

_____

_____

Stress Management Self-Care Checklist

On a scale of 1 to 10, rank the level of stress you feel right now:

What is the biggest source of stress in your life today?

○ **Work**   1 2 3 4 5 6 7 8 9 10

Is there a clear separation between work and home? Are you frustrated with your colleagues or boss? Are the expectations at work set impossibly high?

○ **Family**   1 2 3 4 5 6 7 8 9 10

Is there division in your family? Are you having a difficult time adjusting to family changes? Is there a lack of communication between parents, siblings, partners, or kids?

○ **Conflict**   1 2 3 4 5 6 7 8 9 10

Are there any unresolved conflicts in your life right now? Are there recurring disagreements at work or with loved ones? Are both sides willing to achieve a peaceful resolution?

○ **Money**   1 2 3 4 5 6 7 8 9 10

Is money causing tension in your relationships? Are you finding it difficult to pay the bills and provide a quality life for your family? Are you having a difficult time agreeing on a financial plan or budget?

○ **Illness**   1 2 3 4 5 6 7 8 9 10

Are you (or someone you love) suffering from disease, illness or a loss of a loved one? Are you having a difficult time concentrating or completing day-to-day tasks due to an illness? Are you getting the medical care and attention you need and deserve?

○ **Other**   1 2 3 4 5 6 7 8 9 10

Are you having a difficult time articulating your thoughts and feelings? Are you seeking to control an uncontrollable situation? Are you able to minimize stress by planning and organizing ahead of time?

Stress Management Self-Reflection Exercise

When completing this stress management self-reflection exercise, always ask yourself:

◉ Why am I feeling stressed, anxious, overwhelmed, or worried about this issue?
◉ Am I thinking about the problem or am I focused on a solution?
◉ How do I define a healthy, happy, and lasting resolution to this stress?
◉ Who can I turn to for help?
◉ What will I do, today, to find a better way?

Work Stress

Work provides a means to live; nothing more, nothing less.

Take things one day at a time, but always make time for your most important asset: YOU!

REFLECTION:

_____
_____
_____
_____
_____
_____
_____
_____
_____

Family Stress

Regardless of past pain or conflict, family is still family. By showing respect and honoring one another, you are doing all you can to be a positive role model for others.

REFLECTION:

_____
_____
_____
_____
_____
_____
_____
_____

Stress Management Self-Reflection Exercise

When completing this stress management self-reflection exercise, always ask yourself:

⊙ Why am I feeling stressed, anxious, overwhelmed, or worried about this issue?
⊙ Am I thinking about the problem or am I focused on a solution?
⊙ How do I define a healthy, happy, and lasting resolution to this stress?
⊙ Who can I turn to for help?
⊙ What will I do, today, to find a better way?

Conflict

Unresolved conflicts can deeply affect your sleep, diet, and physical or mental health. Choose peace, even if it means you have to admit your mistakes or make some compromises.

REFLECTION:

_____
_____
_____
_____
_____
_____
_____
_____
_____

Money Stress

A big part of money management is knowing where the money is going. By trimming your budget, living on cash, and documenting all purchases, you'll always be aware of your money. If skill development is necessary to boost your income, then save up for your education before spending your money on things you really don't need.

REFLECTION:

_____
_____
_____
_____
_____
_____
_____
_____

Stress Management Self-Reflection Exercise

When completing this stress management self-reflection exercise, always ask yourself:

- Why am I feeling stressed, anxious, overwhelmed, or worried about this issue?
- Am I thinking about the problem or am I focused on a solution?
- How do I define a healthy, happy, and lasting resolution to this stress?
- Who can I turn to for help?
- What will I do, today, to find a better way?

Illness

Sometimes the only thing we can do is accept the challenges in our lives as opportunities for learning and growth. Time heals all wounds of the heart, mind, and soul. By seeking the support of others, you will see the truth: you're not alone! After all, with love, patience, and prayer you can accomplish great things.

REFLECTION:

_____

_____

_____

_____

_____

_____

_____

_____

_____

Other

Stress adds a whole new level of complexity into your day. Only focus on the things you can control in the moment because there's nothing more you can do other than your best. If it's between reacting rashly or patiently to a stressful situation, always choose patience. You'll thank yourself later!

REFLECTION:

_____

_____

_____

_____

_____

_____

_____

SELF CARE

In the boxes, describe and draw practical ways you can show yourself care

DAILY ACTION PLANNING SHEET

MAJOR GOAL

TODAY'S 3 MAJOR TASKS

1. _____
   _____
2. _____
   _____
3. _____
   _____

NOTES:

TODAY'S 3 MINOR TASKS

1. _____
   _____
2. _____
   _____
3. _____
   _____

NOTES:

IDEA DUMP ZONE
(TO DEAL WITH LATER)

_____
_____
_____
_____
_____
_____
_____
_____
_____
_____
_____
_____
_____
_____
_____
_____
_____
_____
_____
_____
_____
_____
_____
_____

DAILY ACTION PLANNING SHEET

MAJOR GOAL

IDEA DUMP ZONE
(TO DEAL WITH LATER)

_____
_____
_____
_____
_____
_____
_____
_____
_____
_____
_____
_____
_____
_____
_____
_____
_____
_____
_____
_____
_____
_____
_____

TODAY'S 3 MAJOR TASKS

1. _____
   _____
2. _____
   _____
3. _____
   _____

NOTES:

TODAY'S 3 MINOR TASKS

1. _____
   _____
2. _____
   _____
3. _____
   _____

NOTES:

DAILY ACTION PLANNING SHEET

MAJOR GOAL

IDEA DUMP ZONE
(TO DEAL WITH LATER)

_____

TODAY'S 3 MAJOR TASKS

1. _____

_____

2. _____

_____

3. _____

_____

NOTES:

TODAY'S 3 MINOR TASKS

1. _____

_____

2. _____

_____

3. _____

_____

NOTES:

DAILY ACTION PLANNING SHEET

MAJOR GOAL

TODAY'S 3 MAJOR TASKS

1. _____
   _____
2. _____
   _____
3. _____
   _____

NOTES:

TODAY'S 3 MINOR TASKS

1. _____
   _____
2. _____
   _____
3. _____
   _____

NOTES:

IDEA DUMP ZONE
(TO DEAL WITH LATER)

_____
_____
_____
_____
_____
_____
_____
_____
_____
_____
_____
_____
_____
_____
_____
_____
_____
_____
_____
_____
_____
_____
_____
_____

DAILY ACTION PLANNING SHEET

MAJOR GOAL

IDEA DUMP ZONE
(TO DEAL WITH LATER)

_____
_____
_____
_____
_____
_____
_____
_____
_____
_____
_____
_____
_____
_____
_____
_____
_____
_____
_____
_____
_____
_____
_____

TODAY'S 3 MAJOR TASKS

1. _____
   _____
2. _____
   _____
3. _____
   _____

NOTES:

TODAY'S 3 MINOR TASKS

1. _____
   _____
2. _____
   _____
3. _____
   _____

NOTES:

DAILY ACTION PLANNING SHEET

MAJOR GOAL

IDEA DUMP ZONE
(TO DEAL WITH LATER)

TODAY'S 3 MAJOR TASKS

1. _____
   _____
2. _____
   _____
3. _____
   _____

NOTES:

TODAY'S 3 MINOR TASKS

1. _____
   _____
2. _____
   _____
3. _____
   _____

NOTES:

DAILY ACTION PLANNING SHEET

MAJOR GOAL

TODAY'S 3 MAJOR TASKS

1. _____

_____

2. _____

_____

3. _____

_____

NOTES:

TODAY'S 3 MINOR TASKS

1. _____

_____

2. _____

_____

3. _____

_____

NOTES:

IDEA DUMP ZONE
(TO DEAL WITH LATER)

_____

_____

_____

_____

_____

_____

_____

_____

_____

_____

_____

_____

_____

_____

_____

_____

_____

_____

_____

_____

_____

DAILY ACTION PLANNING SHEET

MAJOR GOAL

IDEA DUMP ZONE
(TO DEAL WITH LATER)

_____

_____

_____

TODAY'S 3 MAJOR TASKS

_____

1. _____

_____

_____

2. _____

_____

_____

3. _____

_____

_____

NOTES:

_____

_____

_____

_____

TODAY'S 3 MINOR TASKS

_____

_____

1. _____

_____

_____

2. _____

_____

_____

3. _____

_____

NOTES:

_____

_____

_____

Weekly Planner

Monday

Tuesday

Wednesday

Thursday

Friday

To-do

Notes

Weekly Planner

Monday

Tuesday

Wednesday

Thursday

Friday

To-do

Notes

Weekly Planner

Monday

Tuesday

Wednesday

Thursday

Friday

To-do

Notes

Weekly Planner

Monday

Tuesday

Wednesday

Thursday

Friday

To-do

Notes

Weekly Planner

Monday

Tuesday

Wednesday

Thursday

Friday

To-do

Notes

Weekly Planner

Monday

Tuesday

Wednesday

Thursday

Friday

To-do

Notes

Weekly Planner

Monday

Tuesday

Wednesday

Thursday

Friday

To-do

Notes

Weekly Planner

Monday

Tuesday

Wednesday

Thursday

Friday

To-do

Notes

Weekly Planner

Monday

Tuesday

Wednesday

Thursday

Friday

To-do

Notes

Weekly Planner

Monday

Tuesday

Wednesday

Thursday

Friday

To-do

Notes

Weekly Planner

Monday

Tuesday

Wednesday

Thursday

Friday

To-do

Notes

Self Note
To My future Self

Please Do:

_____
_____
_____
_____
_____
_____

Please Don't Do:

_____
_____
_____
_____
_____

Self Note
To My future Self

Please Do:

_____

_____

_____

_____

_____

_____

Please Don't Do:

_____

_____

_____

_____

_____

_____

WHAT AM I GOING TO DO NEXT?:

_____

_____

_____

_____

_____

_____

_____

_____

_____

_____

_____

_____

WHAT AM I GOING TO DO NEXT?:

_____

_____

_____

_____

_____

_____

_____

_____

_____

_____

_____

_____

_____

_____

Notes

Notes

Notes

_____

_____

_____

_____

_____

_____

_____

_____

_____

_____

_____

_____

_____

_____

Notes

Notes

Notes

Notes

Notes

Notes

Notes

_____

_____

_____

_____

_____

_____

_____

_____

_____

_____

_____

_____

_____

Notes

Notes

Notes

"You have the power to protect your peace "

It's not selfish to love yourself, take care of yourself, and to make your happiness a priority. It's necessary." – Unknown